SOL'S STORY

The story of a boy who not only survived –
but thrived.

Sol F. Schönberg Laufer

With
Saul Rudman
&
Gabrielle Tudin

Writers' Note: Though this is a work of nonfiction, due to the effects of time and trauma, the authors cannot guarantee that the names, characters, places, and incidents are all entirely accurate. Some details have been changed in order to protect the privacy or dignity of the persons involved.

DEDICATED TO MY BELOVED PARENTS, JONAH AND RACHEL, AND MY SIBLINGS FELAH, HIRSCHEL, AND NACHUM SCHONBERG, A MESSAGE FROM YOUR SOLE SURVIVING SON AND BROTHER:

TAKE SOLACE IN THE PROFOUND STRENGTH AND RESILIENCE INSPIRED BY YOUR LIVES AND EMBODIED IN THIS MEMORIAL WALL. THE EXISTENCE OF THE NEXT GENERATIONS SERVES AS LIVING PROOF THAT THE FLICKER OF YOUR SOULS SHINES BRIGHTER. GENERATIONS YET TO COME WILL KNOW BEYOND DOUBT THAT THE EVIL THAT BRUTALLY STOLE YOUR LIVES FAILED TO EXTINGUISH YOUR FLAMES. YOU WILL NEVER BE FORGOTTEN.

YOUR EVER-LOVING SON AND BROTHER, SOL

Dedication adapted from engraving on the Donor Wall, Holocaust Memorial Museum, Washington, DC 2014

ACKNOWLEDGMENT

Even those who are closest to me have tended to avoid conversation about my experiences and losses under Nazi occupation. Other than sharing my story with interviewers from the Spielberg Project, and various school groups, my story has stayed private.

Then, in 2014, Gabrielle "Gabi" Tudin, granddaughter to my second wife, Sadie Rudman, expressed interest in interviewing me. The timing was right and Gabi, a bright, inquisitive young lady was the perfect person to break the ice. She asked probing questions and transcribed hours of open and often difficult but liberating and enlightening conversation. This manuscript would not exist without Gabi's initiative and willingness to shine a light into some very dark corners of my childhood.

Later, my wife, Sadie's youngest son, Saul Rudman, offered to share some of Gabi's load. Together, they covered a lot of ground that ultimately led to the book before you right now. Devastatingly, Saul passed away suddenly in 2018 at the age of 55, after a battle with pancreatic cancer. He was taken from this life far too soon, and I miss him every day. Saul and I spent countless hours together in the process of writing this book. He used to say he felt so close to my story, it was as if he could feel every inch of my suffering. Saul was gentle, insightful, empathetic, and so giving; and the telling of my story would not be possible without him.

Gabi and Saul, along with my children and grandchildren, are an encouraging reminder of the capacity and motivation of the generations after mine to carry the torch of remembrance forward in order to avoid repetition of the horrors of the past. They seem to want to grapple with and remember the atrocities that devastated their ancestors; and I, in turn, want to share relevant experiences and lessons taken from my own life in honor of those who were murdered and whose story must forever be told through others.

INTRODUCTION

THE HOLOCAUST MUSEUM IN D.C., Yad Vashem in Israel, The Spielberg Project, along with many hundreds of survivors have meticulously documented their holocaust experiences in published books and on film. Thanks to their courage and dedication, several modern-day holocausts may have been recognized and abbreviated and some, prevented.

The importance of educating today's children isn't lost on Sol. He's spoken before groups of school kids, sharing his experiences during the war years and challenging the conclusions they draw along the way. "So, do you think, after hearing my story, that I was an abused child?"

"The answer is absolutely not. Look at me, listen to me, hear about my family, my career successes, awards, huge achievements as a corporate leader, self-taught optics component wizard, civic leader, philanthropist, sculptor, friend, congregation member, and more. How can someone such as this be the product of an abusive childhood?"

The pages that follow try to shed light on this conundrum: How is it that one who endured a horrendously brutal period of his childhood – a period of devastating loss, violence, deprivation, aloneness and terror, during crucial formative years – somehow held onto his life, his sanity, his dignity, his sense of self and sense of pride, his intellect and his ambition, and let's not forget his health and wonderful sense of humor. By reading his story, the reader fills a sacred role as witness to the horrors of the holocaust. In return, you certainly come away with a fresh outlook on your own life and new-found resilience in the face of adversity.

Like many before you, we hope that you will recognize the incredible power and promise of "leaning into the furious winds" rather than stepping away; of saying Yes and stepping up to challenges, even if it involves "faking it 'til you make it"; "fearing only fear itself"; and, when the clouds finally disappear, learning to laugh like you've never laughed before.

CHAPTER ONE

LIFE IN CZARNÓW: PRE-ANNEXATION

I, Shlomo Felix Schonberg, was born on September 7,

1928 in Czarnów, Poland, of parents Rachel and Jonah

Schonberg. I had one older sister, Fella, as well as two

younger brothers, Herschel ('Hershey') and Nachum. The city

of Czarnów was known by various other names over the years

of occupation and annexation, with the borders often shifting

from Poland to Germany rule. It was also the birthplace of my

parents and grandparents, and a hub of Orthodox Jewish

culture and religious practice throughout the centuries.

At the time, Czarnów was located in east-central Poland's Warsaw West County, home to a little over 100,000 people, in a county that covered roughly 205 square miles. The village was a reasonable distance of 21 miles to the east of Warsaw, somewhat remote yet connected enough to foster good commerce and interaction with the wider world. As it turned out, Czarnów had the unfortunate distinction of sitting right on the border of Poland and Germany, with my family home located on what would be the highway traversed by the invading armies.

My mother was one of ten children. With nine brothers, she was the only daughter. Most of her siblings lived in Germany, and most worked in business. Her father, my grandfather, was Nachum Laufer. He had one brother and eight sisters, most of whom lived in Poland. Nachum's wife, my maternal grandmother, was from the Mandelbaum family.

The Mandelbaums were all light-haired, a trait which if anything served me well during the war as a prisoner. The Laufer side of the family were darker-haired, more typical of the Jewish people at that time. I know of only a few from my mother's side of the family who were in concentration camps and survived: a cousin, who survived Germany and died in Israel, and his uncle Joe. Some were smart enough to escape Germany early and go to the east side of the region where the Russians were.

When, in 1941, the Germans attacked the Russians, my family who had taken refuge there were moved to Siberia. One of my uncles with his pregnant wife gave birth to a daughter there, and eventually ended up in Israel. Another uncle was taken alone to Siberia and also survived. He remarried and also ended up in Israel. The rest of my mother's family, to my knowledge, disappeared in the war.

My father had a very tight-knit family, with three brothers and four sisters. My grandfather died when I was a young child. My grandmother herself lived very comfortably, often sending money to the poor. I remember my grandmother had a 'welfare system,' where she would bake challahs and make meals for underprivileged families each Friday, and my sister and I would deliver them.

My father's family were Orthodox Chassidic Jews, going back ten generations. One of the first few generations on his father's side was Yosef Schonberg. Yosef had seven sons and was in the lumber business in Germany and Poland. He owned a large area of forest and supplied all lumber to coal mines. He was a large man in both stature and reputation, and owned his own coach with four horses.

I don't know the names of all of my great-great-grandfather's children, but one of his sons, Meir, had a son Yukel. Yukel was known to be a very bright young man and married the daughter of the first rabbi in Czarnów. Yukel and his wife had a son, Shlomo, who would be my great-grandfather; his son, Moses, my grandfather; and Moses's son, Jonah, was my father. My father wasn't a fanatical Chassid, like some in his family were before him.

Some time ago after the war, around 1970, my cousin Solly who survived the war in England got a letter from one of their uncles in Berlin. This uncle was maybe 90 or 95 years old at the time. He had found out Solly was alive, and wrote a letter to him about the family. The first Schonberg, he shared, was expelled from Germany and went across the border to Poland. He was a scholar, and very wealthy. He came to Poland with his seven sons.

Over the years, two of the seven sons stayed in Poland, and five returned to Germany. I remember from the five who went to Germany, one was a general in the German army, one was a composer and one was a founder of the company Shell. The Shell founder once came to visit his cousins in Poland. He told them he was their cousins, that he was wealthy and had shares of Shell to give to his cousins. His cousins turned him away because he wasn't religious enough for them.

My parents themselves were an ambitious and entrepreneurial couple. I have fond memories of regular visits from my home across the nearby border to Germany, where my parents owned and operated a small food department store. Their store specialized in fresh and dried fruits, imported and domestic cheeses, butter and eggs, and much more. My mother managed the brick and mortar store in Germany, while my father managed a highly successful specialty food distribution business in Poland.

In addition to the retail and wholesale distribution businesses, they owned and operated a small deli restaurant which served standard deli fare, along with an abundance of tasty fruits and sweets.

All of their operations catered to different demographics, but offered the same imported and domestic foods. My father traveled extensively around Poland, selling dairy items to retailers. The businesses and customers benefitted in part from efficiency and economy of scale. For example, they purchased butter in bulk and repackaged it in customer-preferred amounts, using equipment that they purchased for this purpose.

They accomplished the same win-win outcomes through import of large wheels of cheese from Amsterdam. Machines in the store cut the wheels and packaged the resulting bricks for resale. Delicious fresh fruits were bulk purchased and shipped to the store courtesy of an uncle in Germany who specialized in the fresh fruits market.

During a 1995 visit to Poland, I returned to the site of my parents' Polish business. Business was still as it was before the war. I asked for permission to go downstairs to see if it was the same as I remembered. Sure enough, the cellar still housed a few machines, used by my parents to make the delicious syrup and jam that was sold upstairs and in Germany so many years before.

On that same visit, I traveled a few miles down the road from Czarnów to the area once known as "Oświęcim," renamed Auschwitz by the Third Reich. Throughout my life, I have been driven by a pledge that many children make to their parents and grandparents: a commitment to making them proud through good works, good deeds, and success.

Yet in my case, my pledge to my siblings, parents, grandmother, and many more, was to "live *for* them." I dedicated my body and works to their unfulfilled dreams and ambitions.

CHAPTER TWO

1939-1942: INVASION OF POLAND – LIFE TORN APART

It was the summer of 1939, and I was excited for a change of pace and scenery. To me, my younger brother, Herschel, and friends from the area, summer camp in the mountains was synonymous with two exciting, carefree months; and we could taste the mountain springs and delicious breezes awaiting us. I was mostly oblivious to the place and time surrounding us.

The upstairs living room window of my family's apartment overlooked the main street of Czarnów, soon to transform into surreal and terrifying sights unlike any before or since. The universe placed me, my two brothers and sister, and my father and mother, at the center of the crime scene of the century. But none of that existed in the glow of the beckoning summer camp.

The height of my excitement was more than matched by the devastating disappointment I suddenly faced upon learning that plans for the summer had suddenly changed: We were being sent home four weeks early. Hitler was on the move, and "war" was in the air. Herschel and I, along with six other boys from our village, headed home.

Soon after, my parents loaded the whole family onto a horse-drawn wagon, borrowed from a family friend. We stopped to pick up my mother's mother at her home nearby and set out to a farm away from the city. The tension on their faces made it clear that this was not a vacation.

First though, my parents gathered us together for a family meeting, possibly the last of its kind for us. They paired us up and assigned us surrogate parent roles, much like a "buddy system." I, for example, was tasked with looking out for my younger brother, Herschel, should we get separated from our parents.

They then went about sewing money into the clothes and name tags onto the clothes that we were wearing.

I didn't know what to make of it at the time. In hindsight, being a parent and grandparent myself, my heart aches for the crossroads that my family was at, and for the positive, constructive, courageous and honest steps that our parents were taking in the face of looming danger from a known threat. Despite being forced to surrender their businesses and being expelled from Germany, and despite mounting tensions between Poland and Germany, they tried to take whatever proactive, constructive steps they could think of to protect their children.

Even at age 13, I was impressed by their drive to leave no stone unturned and their instinct to do the best one can with the hand one is dealt. In later years their ethic emerged in my own approach to problem solving and managing people.

Much of my success can be traced to my determination to do the same in my tireless effort to do better today than yesterday and even better tomorrow than today. But these were not the only heroic acts of my family during the war; far from it. My aunt, Hannah, acted fearlessly to protect her family from the impending danger:

When the war erupted in 1939, my uncle (one of my mother's nine brothers) Ya'akov was in Italy. He was a fruit broker who traveled far and wide, frequently, buying fruit to ship back to Poland and Germany. He was, in fact, a regular source of specialty fruits that were sold in my parents' businesses.

He was unable to return to his wife, Hannah, and son, Nachum, but he was able to secure official documentation that would allow Hannah and Nachum to leave Germany and join him in Italy. From there, he'd somehow arranged passage on a ship headed to Israel.

When Hannah received the travel authorizations, her son, Nachum, got extremely sick. Hannah knew that taking him to any hospital was extremely dangerous, but his suffering was an equally real threat. She made the decision to have him examined at a Catholic hospital, where he was confined to bed rest and any travel plans for the near future had to be scrapped.

She knew that neither of them stood a chance without travel papers. Even then, safe passage wasn't a sure thing. Still, she decided to take a direct approach to solving the problem of expired documents. Once she was reasonably certain that Nachum was on the mend, Hannah made her way to Gestapo headquarters. Most Jews of sane mind avoided the Gestapo under all and any circumstances; but Hannah wasn't just any person. She was fierce. She'd already concluded that she had little to lose except for her life and Nachum's, and that was quickly emerging as the inevitable outcome.

Hannah stood before a senior Gestapo officer, made her case, and demanded that he take care of the situation. She was indignant and apparently made quite a scene, demanding explanations and an apology, which is exactly what she got, in lieu of getting arrested and sent off to an extermination camp. Nachum and his heroic mom were issued new travel documents. They finally started on their trip to Italy, arriving at their destination port.

That was when Hannah learned that Ya'akov was no longer in Italy. Not knowing what had happened to his wife and son when they failed to arrive as planned, he assumed the worst; that they had both been detained and probably imprisoned or murdered by the Nazis. The window of opportunity to escape Europe was barely open at that point, so he boarded the ship bound for Israel, confident that they would follow if, by some miracle, they survived.

Recognizing that the waves of refugees were already overwhelming any safe transportation heading to Israel, Hannah and Nachum boarded a train heading as far away from Hitler's Germany and the invaded countries as possible.

They ultimately made their way to India, where they lived for several years while awaiting visas to start their lives anew in Israel. In the interim, Ya'akov joined the family in India, where their second child, Rosi, was born.

Hannah and Ya'akov and their children represent and symbolize so much hope and healing for a family and a people, brutally decimated by the Nazis. The family put down roots in Israel, where both Nachum and Rosi married and raised families. Nachum and his wife, Zilli, have been blessed with 3 children and grandchildren. Rosi and her husband, David, have 2 children and 5 grandchildren.

One cannot even begin to imagine the riches that the children and grandchildren of over 6 million European Jews would be sharing with the world, today, were they not slaughtered during the Holocaust. For that reason and so many more, the courage shown by Hannah and so many other heroes who saved their children from murder, is a gift to the future and a gift in the present to every human who recognizes that the extinction of the Jewish people would be a devastating blow for humanity. Imagine a world without Einstein, Freud, Perlman, and so many more in any and every walk of life.

With each child saved and each family born, there is the promise of a legacy of meaningful contribution to humanity as long as humanity exists. Sadly, the unfolding events surpassed anything that my parents or any civilized human being could have anticipated.

During our one-week absence at the farm, the German army had invaded Poland, moved the borders, and established full control, with little, if any resistance from the Polish army. Apparently, horse-drawn cannons were no threat to the advancing German military hardware.

Once we got word that we had a home to return to, we started the trip right into the mouth of the dragon. Without much conversation, we loaded up the wagon and started back down the road toward Czarnów. I believe that afternoon was the first time I'd heard gunfire. Our farmer host stopped the cart, spoke with another traveler, and was clearly upset when he returned to inform us that he would need to change our route back to town. He'd learned that the gunfire in the distance was coming from German soldiers along the road up ahead.

We arrived back at home; an upper floor apartment on the main road leading into Czarnów. From the large living room windows and balcony, I had a clear view of the endless streams of German soldiers and military vehicles that poured into Poland.

Within a day of our return from the farm, my aunt burst into the apartment, sobbing unlike anyone I'd heard before. I overheard much of the agonized conversation. Her two very handsome, bright, loving sons were among a group of roughly 100 Jewish boys and men who were randomly stopped along the road leading to and from town. This happened the prior afternoon around the same time that we were stopped by the sound of gunshots in the distance.

The soldiers forced them to dig a shallow trough beside the road, lined them up in front of their freshly dug grave, and shot them in successive batches. Each subsequent group would cover the prior group with dirt before lining up to be shot, and covered, only partially, with the dirt they'd excavated.

A single bullet did not ensure a perfect kill; but rather than ensuring their victims were dead and firing again at close range, they buried them in a shallow grave and issued strict orders that the site and victims be left to bleed to death. Witnesses who traveled that road reported seeing the blood drenched earth beside the road moving and hearing it groaning for hours, if not days, after the mass execution.

The vision of my two innocent cousins' bloody hands reaching from shallow grave as their friends, family, and neighbors were forced to file past them, unable to come to their rescue, haunts and enrages me to this very day.

Suddenly, we had been introduced to the cruel brutality of the Nazis and there was no escaping the paralyzing terror that they wanted us to feel. The writing on the wall seemed clear… these murderers were sociopathic, cruel, sadistic, and capable of unimaginable horrors. We, the Jews and other "undesirables" were in dire straits. Uprisings and resistance seemed entirely impossible and futile under such circumstances.

As my mother tried to console my grieving aunt, I overheard her say, "Your sons were righteous people. They were good boys. God took them early so they shouldn't suffer because, in the end, the Germans will murder all of us."

A few months after the roadside execution, members of the Jewish community petitioned the city government for permission to exhume the remains in order to give them a proper burial in the Jewish cemetery. Permission was granted. I was present to witness the opening of the mass grave and removal of the badly decomposed corpses. Each was placed in a wooden box which was then sealed with tar before the somber procession of 100 caskets made its way to the cemetery. They were laid to rest in a large grave which was covered with tombstones before the day was over.[1]

The Germans fought the psychological war as effectively as the war fought with munitions. They planned and executed those plans with remarkable efficiency and determination. Were it not for the Allied forces and the

---

[1] A few months after the roadside execution and burial of 100 or more people, members of the Jewish community petitioned the city government for permission to exhume the remains in order to give them a proper burial in the Jewish cemetery. Permission was granted. I was present to witness the opening of the mass grave and removal of the badly decomposed corpses. Each was placed in a wooden box which was then sealed with tar before the somber procession of 100 caskets made its way to the cemetery. They were laid to rest in a large grave which was covered with tombstones before the day was over.

Russian Army bringing their rampage to an end, the relatively few surviving Jews, myself included, and other persecuted groups would not have held on much longer.

So, we come full circle to the heroes who knowingly or unknowingly saved my life and the lives of others, even in the early days of the annexation of my homeland: My parents, Jonah and Rachel Schonberg, who taught me to keep trying until I found a way forward... to never give up and always seek constructive steps, always looking ahead. I am eternally grateful for their heroism in the face of chaos and insanity.

And the farmer friend of my Father, who opened his heart and home when our family needed to prepare for the worst and enjoy the peace of nature together one last time. His caring and willingness to "go the extra mile" through the woods spared the lives of my father, brothers, Herschel and Nachum and myself that Autumn afternoon in 1939. For that, I am eternally grateful.

Sometime later in 1941, we were forced to give up our beautiful apartment and move to the ghetto. The apartment was on the top floor of a building on the main boulevard that brought the invading Nazi army across the nearby border into the newly-annexed Poland. I used to kneel on the sofa and peer down at the troops and military vehicles, sheltered from the gravity of the scene by my seemingly calm parents and nanny.

My safe perch was gone, confiscated in much the same brutal manner as my parents' meticulously assembled and managed businesses. The first to go was the store over the border in German territory. My mother would commute to manage the highly successful specialty foods import business.

Their first store, right in Czarnów, survived a bit longer. Then, like the store in Germany, they were forced to "sell" the business to German gentile buyers for a token few coins. In true German attention to details and appearances, the forced transfer from Jew to Gentile was handled as a formal transaction, complete with the exchange of signatures and currency, albeit equivalent to a couple of dollars.

Not surprisingly, when an edict came down, forcing similar surrender ("sale") of Jewish-owned businesses in Poland, the same party that purchased the German store came to Czarnów, pennies and pens in hand, ready to relieve my parents of their business. To their credit, they made an allowance in the transaction for my father to occupy a cubicle in the store office… a place for him to conduct whatever little venture they supposed he may be able to launch.

By the time they came to evict my family from our home, nothing came as a surprise, given what had happened with my parents' source of livelihood. We diligently moved to the ghetto. It was not a good section of town. The buildings were old and largely unmaintained. My family was assigned to a single room in a small apartment which we shared with many other families.

Somehow, seven of us lived in one room. My parents slept in a small closet storage area, leaving my grandmother and four children to share the rest of the room. The plumbing and water supply weren't connected or were broken. All activities of daily living that required water, whether hygiene, cooking, toilets, required a visit to the outdoors.

The same proud, respected, generous grandmother, around 75 years old, who lovingly prepared and distributed meals for the sick and the needy every Friday, shared this cold, crowded space with four grandchildren and her own son and daughter-in-law. Still, there was unwavering dedication to maintaining an air of calm, constructive, care and camaraderie. Even when it seemed impossible to salvage a shred of self-esteem or self-worth, my grandmother and parents managed to come to the rescue.

Somehow, I became the one and only person entrusted with the delicate task of trimming Grandma's hair. Her wig, also known as a "sheitle," was part and parcel of the orthodox Jewish woman's public life. Looking presentable and feeling comfortable required regular attention to her "real" hair. Only I was trusted with this responsibility.

From time to time there were rumors that there would be house to house raids to purge the ghetto of the elderly and the sick Jews. Those nights, I would scramble down a home-made rickety ladder that descended to a potato cellar beneath the floor of our ghetto home. My father steadied the ladder up above, as my grandmother quietly descended to her bitterly cold, dark, lonely refuge for yet another night.

The ghetto was ostensibly "open." There were no high walls or gates, but that did not mean that there weren't any restrictions. The Gestapo regularly rounded up respected community leaders, my father included, and detained them for five-day stretches. They served as human collateral: non-refundable deposits in the event that any German soldiers lost their lives to the resistance. Curfews were strictly enforced by the German soldiers who frequently reinforced rules by example. Their strategy was brutally effective.

On one such occasion, seven Jews were accused of violating the curfew. They had disobeyed the rules, albeit by a few minutes. The entire ghetto population was summoned to a nearby park. This was the one place that featured a tree large enough to suspend seven adult corpses from a single tree limb.

On one side of the lifeless corpses were the community for whom the collective punishment had been arranged. On the other side of the tree, camped out on their picnic blankets and lawn chairs, town's people from beyond the ghetto, celebrating their good fortune, now that they were free to "take back" the homes of the Jews who were now in the ghetto.

The music was barbarically cheerful and did little to mask the sounds of clinking beers and roaring laughter that erupted all seven times that a human ornament was choked by their hastily-improvised noose, offering several minutes of terrifying writhing, self-soiling "entertainment" for a drunk audience. I stood watching as the arc of the branch as each successive person's weight was transferred from a platform to the tree. With each successive execution, the twisting corpse's feet came closer and closer to the ground. By the seventh hanging, the feet of some could just barely touch the soiled earth.

A young, distraught child emerged from the ghetto witnesses and approached the lifeless body of his father who was within reach now. He wept bitterly and begged repeatedly for his father to come down now. But that was not the plan. For 24 hours we remained there, forced to observe the consequences of any failure to obey the rules of our captors.

I made a point of revisiting that horrific site in 1995. The hanging tree was still there, surrounded by homes. I was surprised to find a commemoration plaque, honoring the memories of the seven Jews whose lives were so brutally snuffed out at that site. I learned that a school nearby takes responsibility for placing fresh flowers at the tree each and every week. Even in the darkest corners of the crime scene, there were embers of rebirth and healing.

While standing and reflecting on this place and time that had haunted every day of my life, I was interrupted by a lady who stepped up beside me. She saw my tears and inquired whether any of the seven victims were family. I responded: "No, but I lived here at the time." She hesitated and then offered that she, too, had lived in town at the time and still did.

"I can't get the picture out of my mind. Each time I go by this place I see those poor people hanging." I was touched by the magnitude of the tragedy and the myriad of random twists and turns of fate that could so easily have cut my own life short before it barely got going, and by the flicker of recognition and responsibility that the plaque, flowers, and local resident represented on that agonizing return to the scene of the crime.

CHAPTER THREE
1942-1945: LOSS AND SURVIVAL

By 1942, we all knew what was happening in Auschwitz. Everyone was afraid we would be next. By the end of the year, I remember it was getting very cold, and the SS had been doing nightly raids. They went from home to home, room to room, dragging people out and assembling them in a big soccer field in town.

Knowing they were coming, we hid my grandmother in a hole in our basement. We were taken with the others to the field. We stayed there overnight, freezing, with only one blanket to keep us warm. In the morning, each family was seen by a commission of the Gestapo SS, who made selections on who to send to camps. The SS men recognized my mother from her business in Germany and told her, in German, that one of us had to go.

Of course, they looked to my father – but I jumped in front of him and begged them to take me in his place. I pleaded, "My father is not a healthy man, please take me." They asked, "Are you sure you want to go to the camp?" I didn't hesitate. This was the last time I saw my parents. I was fourteen years old.

The following day, I was transported to Blechhammer, a forced labor camp for Jews, and part of the Auschwitz complex. The camp provided laborers for a number of industries in Upper Silesia, the most prized of which was the production of synthetic fuel, desperately needed for the German war effort. The allies repeatedly bombed the complex and it was rebuilt each time. Many hundreds of prisoners lost their lives during the allied bombings of the fuel production plant. In addition to several thousand male prisoners, some 200 Jewish women were held at Blechhammer. The total number of forced laborers working in all camps at Blechhammer and surroundings reached about 48,000 people by 1944. This included about 2,000 British Prisoners of war.

All the workers there were slaves. There were prisoners of war, Jews, and Germans alike. We wore black and white striped uniforms, and each Sunday they would cut a strip of hair down the middle of our heads so that if we ever ran away, everyone would know we were a prisoner.

I had several jobs at the camp. Supplies for converting coal to airplane fuel would come to the camp by river on boats, and I would unload the boats and carry sacks of concrete to the trucks on my back. I would also dig roads in the streets. This was all hard work for a child of fourteen years old. We went to work mostly by foot each day. Each morning, we got up, dressed in our uniforms, and each worker was called up by number and assigned a job for the day.

They gave us 'coffee' to drink before work, which was really a roasted wheat. At work, they gave us thirty minutes to pause for 'lunch,' which was a small pot of soup for all of us to share. We slept in a small barrack filled with maybe 40 people. There were three levels of bunks, with one door and window on one of the walls. I remember being the youngest in this room – perhaps in the entire camp. When we came back from working each day, we were very tired, and always talking about what we missed from the good days at home… what we would eat if we could.

There is one moment I remember so clearly to this day. It was our first Yom Kippur imprisoned in the camps. We all gathered on the floor of our barrack, maybe forty of us, sitting together in a semi-circle. One of the prisoners was an Ashkenazi cantor. He had a beautiful voice. He chanted the *Kol Nidre* prayers, and we followed along with his words.

Some of the older men knew the prayers by heart. As long as I live, I will never forget this moment. All of us were crying. Even today, each year on Yom Kippur I have tears in my eyes remembering this painful night.

After being at Blechhammer for a time, I remember a dysentery outbreak that was pervasive and lethal. It got so bad that they eventually decided to shut the whole camp down completely and we were all sent off to other labor camps, or death camps. I was moved four times after Blechhammer, which turned out to be one of the 'better' prisons. Yes, it turns out that hell comes in various flavors. They transferred me to 'Brandau' for a short time, and soon on to Zwittau – the birthplace of Oskar Schindler, who saved 1,200 Jews working at his factory during the war.

The camp in Zwittau was one of the 'nicer' camps of the three years, in the city center surrounded with wired fencing. The camp buildings were literally across the street from where people lived. They taught me to be a weaver there, and I worked in a large textile company at night, operating the machines. In the day time, civilians worked there. The cook at the camp was a man named Pinchas Goldwasser. He was in his 30s, Chassidic, and knew my parents from living in a city nearby to us. He was very kind to me. He would allow me to go into the kitchen and get the scraps from the dirty pots.

It was a good camp, comparatively. We played soccer against the guards, and neighbors across the street would cheer and watch. One Sunday the guards even took the workers to see the city. One day, I noticed some food in my basket at my work station. I took it and wrote little note in German saying thank you for the food. The anonymous gifter replied to me, writing that I would see more from time to time. I never did meet this man.

Soon after, though, I asked him for a favor: I had written a letter to my nanny from home, and asked him to please mail it to her with his own address included – in hopes that she would reply. She did, but not with good news. She wrote that my cousin was also taken to a concentration camp, and my parents were sent to Auschwitz, along with my brothers, and my sister was also sent to a camp. She said that he should not expect further communication from her, since it was too dangerous, and she was too afraid.

At some point, I'm not sure when, they moved me to a different camp in Germany, called Faulbrück. Faulbrück was one of 70 sub-camps of the Gross-Rosen concentration camp. In total, 125,000 prisoners passed through Gross-Rosen; 40,000 perished. Faulbrück was a horrible camp. When I arrived, I was told my uncle David died here, as well as the brother-in-law of my father. It was a nightmare. We slept in a big warehouse, on shelves stacking four or five levels up.

In the middle of the warehouse were two big bowls for us to urinate in. The work was harder than I had experienced in the other camps. It was the same type of work – construction, mostly – but when we went to work each day, we would count how many of us went, and how many of us came back alive.

The food there was terrible. I would volunteer to work in the kitchen, cleaning up the mess and saving some extra scraps to survive on. When we would come back from work each day, we had to stand in line for food. I had a trick that I would use, though. I would get food, turn my hat around to cover my face, and get back in line for seconds.

One time, I was caught. There was a camp leader, a Jew, who saw me sneaking seconds. He asked me how many times I had taken food. I couldn't lie. He called over the German guard, who told the Jew to give me 25 lashings. The Jewish leader took me into a room, laid me down, and tied my hands together. He told me to scream twenty-five times.

The German stood outside, counting the screams. Only once at the end did he hit me, to make the German believe I received all 25 hits.

At some point, another epidemic hit the camp, and I got it. I believe it was typhus. We had nowhere to go for help; we just lay on our shelves waiting to die – no medications, no water. Each morning they came in and took the dead out. That day, I was laying on my shelf, burning with fever. I dreamt that my mother was next to me, putting cold ice and water on my forehead, feeding me my favorite food (a hard roll of salami). I believe the comfort those dreams brought me are what kept me alive. I was weak, I couldn't walk, but I survived.

Another day, when I was recovered, we were waiting for the train to take us to work when I saw across the tracks another open train car, filled with cheese for the Germans. I ran to the car, filled my pockets, and ran back. Everyone asked where I got the cheese and ran to get some for themselves. The guard spotted the group and started hitting them with his rifle. When we went back to the camp later on, he was told to pick out the people he saw stealing the cheese.

We stood in three rows for the lineup. I was second in line. He walked slowly past each of us. He stopped at me and I looked right into his eyes. I prayed silently to myself, 'Please don't pick me. Please don't pick me.' He continued walking through the line. Soon, though, he came back to me. Again, I didn't know what to do, but I looked right into his eyes and waited. That day, five of us were hanged in public and beaten to death. I wasn't one of them.

They closed that subcamp, and I was transferred to another camp called Langenbielau – another Gross-Rosen subcamp. The camp was not as good as Zvitau, but not as bad as Faulbrück. Again, we slept in barracks here. There was some water to wash our faces, but not much more than that hygiene-wise. We were forced to relieve ourselves outside in the ground.

We did the same type of construction work here as in the last camp. We worked together with non-Jewish prisoners, and they would give me some food from their camps. I remember the non-Jews were given better food than us. We were nearing the end of 1944, and at this point, I understood if I didn't have food, I wouldn't survive; so, I did everything in my power to find extra food. I had to do it.

One winter day, at the construction site, there was a nearby field where they were making sugar from red beets. I snuck away to the field and took some beets in my pockets. When I came back to camp I was caught. The guards made me undress and run back and forth outside in the snow until I collapsed. When they brought me back to my barrack, the man who slept above me went to get honey from his sister who was a cook in the next camp over. He fed me some honey and massaged my limbs to warm me up, saving me from frostbite and surely death. He saved my life.

Later on, one day, I was taken with a guard to go pick up some tools. As we were walking, I saw an apple tree. I asked the guard if I could take an apple. He said fine, take what's on the ground. As I was gathering the apple, a little girl came out of her house and saw me. She asked her mother in German, 'What is this?' Her mother replied, 'A Jew.' 'This is a Jew?' The girl was surprised – she had thought a Jew was a type of animal.

Another day, the guards in the camp asked for anyone who was a carpenter to step forward. I stood up and said I am a carpenter. The man next to me said, 'Are you crazy? You're not a carpenter!' But I knew it was a long winter, and I would freeze if I kept working outside. I knew that they were building barracks and figured that couldn't be so hard to learn.

I told the guards that I also knew how to do fine carpentry – that my father had a business making furniture. This wasn't true. So why do this? Well, winter was coming, and I knew that warmth would make the difference between life and death. We had no coats in the winter. I would take an empty sack of cement and cut a hole for my head and my arms to keep me warmer and lined my wooden shoes with paper. I also figured that the soldiers needed gifts to send to their families for Christmas. This way, I was assigned a gift-making job and a warm place to work.

I quickly figured out what I needed to know in order to not get detected as a fraud. Was it risky? Yes. But without taking such risks, there's no way I would have survived.

They sent me to work in the place where the carpenters were building barracks for the army. It was indoors – nice and warm. The supervisor there was called the master. He was a big, tough man who didn't like the guards. He took one look at me and said, "You're not Jewish – the guard looks more Jewish than you!" I could tell then that he had a soft spot for me, and I took advantage.

I asked the master one day if he would collect cigarette stubs whenever he saw them around town. He asked me, why? I explained I would take the leftover tobacco from each stub and roll them into new papers, so I could exchange them for food in the camp. The next week, he gave me a coffee cup full of cigarette stubs. The food I got from exchanging these stubs surely saved my life.

CHAPTER FOUR

1945: LIBERATION

The last couple of months before liberation, we sensed something was coming. We would hear the cannons shooting in the distance, but didn't know whether it was the Americans, the Russians, or who else. Liberation Day for us was May 8, 1945. We woke up that morning and suddenly all the guards had disappeared. A Jewish leader of the camp told us there are no more guards, we are free. Everyone cried, hugged, and sang Hatikvah.

The day after the German guards disappeared, a couple of Russian soldiers entered the prison grounds on horseback. I understood enough Russian to know that the war was over, and the prisoners were free to leave; but that was easier said than done. Without strength, clothing, support, communication channels, or homes and loved ones to go to, many survivors needed time to catch up with their newfound freedom.

Over the next few days we found our way into the nearby town of Reichenbach, abandoned by the inhabitants who'd heard the horror stories about the brutality of the Russian army, seeking revenge for the carnage that resulted from the ruthless German people and army.

With the town's people on the run, the survivors came and went like zombies, gathering clothing and food, then meandering back to the prison camp. For many, the scarcity of the past few years made it hard to resist the temptation of the relatively abundant food that was available to them in the town. During the early days after liberation, many died, ironically, from over-indulging their appetites and over-taxing their depleted bodies.

After two or three days of this, the Russians came in and said the camps are closed, and we had to leave. I went back to the city and was taken in by a German family. I lived in their small house and was there for a few days, maybe a week. They fed me and took care of me, until I found out they would receive benefits from housing me. I refused and left.

Soon, I ran in to Pinchas Goldwasser, the cook who helped me in Zwittau. Pinchas had found his nephew, Ya'akov, and said I must come with them. We found an abandoned apartment that must have belonged to a doctor, it was so beautiful. We lived like kings. After maybe two weeks, we heard that there might be help for us in Prague. To make it down to Prague, we needed to go through the mountains; and the only way was on bicycle.

Myself, Pinchas, Ya'akov, and two women bought bikes and started our trek. It was windy and mountainous; and Ruty, one of the girls with us, fell off the road. She was bleeding badly so we stopped at a German home nearby. They took us in, cleaned her face and dressed her wound, and let us sleep there for the night. The next morning, we kept moving towards Prague.

We arrived in Prague to find big buildings to house refugees. Pinchas knew Hebrew, Ya'akov knew English and Hebrew; so, they said we should go to the British Consulate and tell them we are from Palestine and got stuck in Poland during the war. Ya'akov spoke to them in English and told them we wanted to return to Palestine. The Consulate took our names and told us there was a plane that leaves once a week from Prague to Paris with prisoners of war. They gave us a flight date scheduled four weeks from then.

In the meantime, I made plans to make my way back to Czarnów to search for news of my family. We had arranged to leave messages in a pre-arranged location. By the time I arrived and thumbed through the pages, I found nothing from family. I had known that the odds of them surviving the war were almost zero. But the reality was harsh, to say the least.

Now, at the age of 17 and alone in the world, I decided I had to move on. There was nothing to keep me in Poland and no one to tell me what to do. So, along with other young refugees, I boarded a plane from Prague to Paris. From there, I made my way to the port at Marseilles, where I arranged passage on a vessel heading to Israel.

I was detained immediately as I disembarked at Haifa. Once again, I found myself behind barbed wire, this time at the hands of British authorities. My new 'home', Camp Atlit, was one of many detention camps for "displaced persons" aka "D.P.'s," fleeing anti-Semitism and war-ravaged Europe. Their disposition depended on the international communities' willingness to open their borders, hearts, and wallets to the devastated refugees/survivors. Having survived Hitler and lost everything they held dear, the new arrivals temporarily lost their freedom once again.

Camp Atlit was a pivotal place for me. I left Germany, Poland, and France behind, certain that I was the sole survivor of the entire family... that I was entirely alone in this world. To this day, even I marvel at the decisions and actions that I pursued following liberation as such a young boy. In one sense, I had just been through a three-year accelerated course in solo survival and passed with flying colors.

Of the options that I could pursue immediately, Israel seemed most likely to accept undocumented refugees. With assistance from the Israeli Hagenah's agents in France, I had taken the first steps toward a new life in Israel, but anything was still possible, including deportation to Cypress and beyond, as happened with many fellow refugees who had no papers, contacts or sponsors in Israel.

There was a message board when we arrived at Atlit. Israelis seeking surviving relatives and friends posted information, hoping that they would learn something from Atlit refugees or perhaps even find family among the new arrivals. Not long after my arrival, I came across a message from my Uncle David. He came to Atlit searching for me, having been tipped off about my arrival there. In the message, there was an invitation for me to meet him the next day.

The moment I heard my name called out by a friendly voice on the civilian side of the barbed wire fence, everything changed. David Laufer was my mother's closest brother. There was no way that I would have known that my Uncle David had left Austria and established himself in Israel early in the war. Having been forced to surrender his business and its assets, David was riding out the war with hopes of returning to reclaim what was rightfully his back in Europe and Russia.

When he saw me, David immediately recognized his sister in my face; and for a few precious moments, both of us were at once flooded and devastated by long-avoided grief, heartbreaking sorrow, and breathtaking relief.

As it happened, the plight of Jews in detention and D.P. camps back in Europe, in Cypress, and in Israel, caused much friction between the leaders of the allied nations. Tensions reached their peak when British ships blockaded ships carrying refugees to Israel, redirecting them to camps in Cypress and elsewhere. Israel had also received waves of Jewish refugees fleeing persecution in Syria and Lebanon.

They were the earliest residents of the British camp Atlit. Given the massive influx of European and Russian Jews, the British needed to get some refugees out of Atlit. The proposed British solution was to simply return Syrian and Lebanese refugees to their home countries. This was not aligned with Israel's perception of their role as safe haven for diaspora Jews who faced persecution and anti-Semitism.

Against this backdrop, underground groups in Israel and abroad, including the Israeli Hagenah, took matters into their own hands. They continued to smuggle hundreds of illegal immigrants into the country in defiance of the British Authority in Palestine. During a now-famous Hagenah raid on Camp Atlit, the British guards were disarmed, and detainees all fled on foot. After making their way to a kibbutz near Haifa, they were given clothing and various disguises in anticipation of the British hunt for the former detainees. But amongst all of this, I was finally in Israeli society and free.

CHAPTER FIVE

1946-1951: LIFE IN ISRAEL

Over the several next days, my uncle arranged for me to receive an updated (forged) identity card in order to evade the British forces. In the process, I surrendered my given last name in exchange for my mother's maiden name, which I kept throughout my adult life. Sol "Shlomo" Felix Schonberg became Sol Felix Laufer.

My uncle David told me to come stay with him in his apartment, but I said no – I wanted to stay with the people I was used to. I felt more comfortable from the same place as me, who spoke the same language. He said fine, I won't pressure you, and gave me his number to call him when I was ready. Soon after, I finally decided I would go. David sent me money, and I took a cab to his home.

In those times, my uncle was my brother, my father, my friend. When I first arrived, I would guard my food when I ate. But slowly, slowly, David would move my arms away from my plate, one by one, until I no longer guarded my food. I slept on his sofa in the living room, and he would wake me by clapping gently. He sent me back to school, took me to his physician for a full checkup, and fixed my teeth at the dentist. He bought me new clothes and gave me a new life. He did all this without ever asking me what happened.

One Friday night, David invited his good friend, Dr. Cook to join us. I believe he was a psychologist of some kind. The three of us sat outside on David's balcony, and Dr. Cook started gently asking me questions about what happened. He pushed me to keep talking. It was the first time I had ever spoken the words aloud. I cried with him for hours. It was the first time I allowed myself to break down, but it was good for me.

Like everything that I set my mind to, I learned Hebrew fluently and in record time. I integrated quickly, joined the army, fought for the Independence of Israel, and married a *sabra* (native Israeli), named Betty. Once I was in Israel and met these Israeli Jews, I was taken by the spirit of fighting for freedom and independence. I started to question… why didn't any of us fight back?

My early goals were therefore to shed my status and appearance as a refugee survivor in order to fully integrate and be fully embraced in Israeli society. Speaking, reading, and writing the language fluently was an ambitious goal, but one that I set his mind to and accomplished in less than five years.

Life in Israel was still very tough. It was tough because I could not shake what I had lost. My family, friends, my childhood were all gone; but David helped me. He taught me not to associate with my old friends. He introduced me to kids my own age, and I finished school with as normal a life as I could hope for. The principal of the school personally tutored me, and I had a Hebrew tutor to teach me the language. Each day I learned 20 new words. I would study on the bus to and from school, and quickly learned to speak like the other Israelis. I even used my slang to socialize and flirt with girls.

When it came to dating, I set equally tough standards. Above all else, I avoided associating with and dating other Holocaust survivors. Survivors generally didn't have family, and I was determined to establish a family much like anyone else, with grandparents, uncles and aunts, cousins, and the like. I had lost my entire family. The only way my children could be a part of a true family was for me to marry into an intact family.

Betty came with an extended family and our chemistry was perfect, too. Once Betty was confident that I was a good match, she suggested that her parents and I meet. Up until that point, I had successfully hidden my survivor history and Betty hadn't found any reason to suspect that I was a survivor and immigrant. Even so, they accepted me into their family

and we were soon married.

Betty and I at our wedding, 1950

After finishing school, I joined the Israeli army. My service in the Israeli Defense Forces was a perfect springboard into my life. When I was joining the army, I wanted to be a mechanic. I told my father-in-law and asked him to teach me a bit about mechanics. So, when I got to the army, I told them simply I was a mechanic. I passed their test to be a diesel mechanic – having had no license, never having driven a car, and still got 100% on the exam.

They sent me to a tank division to be their mechanic, and with time, I learned how to run a tank, and served as a tank commander for a time. On the tanks, the equipment needed to be calibrated and cleaned. One day, I watched an experience soldier clean the equipment; and the next day, I did it myself. He came and saw my work and asked, who did this? It looks beautiful! I told him it had been me, and he asked how I knew to do this. I said, I saw you doing it, so I tried myself.

From there, they sent me to work at the army laboratory for repairs and calibration of all equipment. The lab was run by Major Plout. He was a very smart guy and used to work for Goldberg Instruments. Goldberg Instruments was run by Professor Emanuel Goldberg, who was the director of Zeiss. The company had sent him to France to work in a smaller branch during the war because they were afraid he would get taken to the camps. From France, he went to Palestine, and the British established a complete lab for the professor to work on military equipment.

When I arrived at the army's lab, I knew nothing… but I learned quickly. After just four or five months, I remember even feeling bored and unchallenged – so the Major told me he would recommend me to work at Goldberg Instruments. I got a job there and sat in their small shop. At the beginning, I simply sat quietly and did my work. Each morning, Professor Goldberg would walk past my desk, say good morning, and shut his door.

One day, the military told us they required some special prisms. The prisms had to be done at 90 degrees exactly, super accurate with a sharp edge. It was very difficult to make. Normally, the army would buy the prisms from India, where they had trained some of the military people to create the prisms by hand, but they needed a larger one this time, and asked Professor Goldberg to do it. The professor assigned me to the job.

For two or three weeks, I sat on a chair in front of a foot peddle machine to run the spindle. By hand, I created this prism; but I also designed a tool to help my hands work the glass more easily. Each day, the professor came by and looked at my work, looked at me, and walked away. When I finally finished the prism, the professor called everyone in the lab over to look at what I had done. He said in his life he had never seen someone sit in the same chair, day after day, and work with such precision.

CHAPTER SIX

1960 - Present: FROM SURVIVING TO THRIVING

Years later, in 1960, George Lowey, a talented engineering colleague and friend of mine at Goldberg Instruments, emigrated to the U.S. with his family. He joined the American Instrument Company (AMINCO) in Silver Springs, Maryland and over time, recruited me to join him and launch a career in the states.

I had been working at Goldberg Instruments for nine or ten years. When I wanted to leave and move my family to America, the professor encouraged me to go. He said I would have more opportunity to develop my skills more in the states than here. We decided to make the move. I got papers set up for myself, Betty, and our two daughters, Rachel, seven years old, and Orna who was around three, and I sold our condominium. Rachel was seven years old at the time and Orna was maybe three or four. We left by ship, disembarking from the port in Haifa. All our family came to see us off, and many of my co-workers came too.

When we arrived in New York, we stayed at a hotel for the weekend. I remember I didn't like New York; it was too noisy and dirty. One day there, Rachel found a gold watch on the street, and I wrote a letter to Betty's parents saying, it's very much true that in America the streets are paved with gold – after just one day we had found gold.

We soon settled in Maryland. Betty devoted herself to parenting and supporting my career. The first winter there was the first time the children had seen snow. I remember Orna woke up and said in Hebrew, 'There's cotton outside! It melted in my hand!' Betty did the parenting while I provided for the family. Soon after moving to America, we had our son, Jonah, or as we call him, "Yonnie."

1960 U.S. Passport

Betty was a vital resource in our home and the community as a whole. Betty was honored with much praise and recognition for her outstanding effort and contribution to numerous charities and boards and was held in high regard in every community that she touched as a volunteer and organizer. My dream at the time was independence: I wanted to establish a company of my own, to own two homes, and to build a life in America.

In my first six months at AMINCO, I worked in manufacturing as a machine operator, but was quickly promoted to supervisor. One day, an outside company in Chicago asked AMINCO if they would produce small roof prisms for them. I asked my boss, should we do it? I know how. He turned me down, claiming we did not do outside work. I asked them if they would allow me to sell my idea for the project to the Chicago company, and they permitted me to do so.

I designed the process of how to make these roof prisms – providing sketches of how to make them efficiently and simply. When I went to Chicago to present them with my idea, I told them they could see my process if they gave me a check first; if they didn't like my idea, I would give the money back. They loved it, and even later called to offer me a job, which I turned down.

After about two years at AMINCO, I was not enjoying the work; it was not challenging enough, and I was not given certain autonomy and freedom to create equipment and processes that I wanted. When my contract was over, and I did not renew. In early 1963, I had read in the paper about a company called Librascope, acquired by General Precision, which was headquarted in Glendale, California and building a branch in Maryland close to NASA to get involved in the space program.

I applied to join the company by phone. I told them I would introduce myself and share my resume only when we met in person. They agreed to a meeting, perhaps because I mentioned Professor Goldberg's name, who had been the director of the well-known company Zeiss. It may have also been my exotic German accent that got me the meet.

After an intense, four-hour interview, Librascope offered me a position. I would buy the equipment I needed for optical manufacturing, hire the necessary talent to open shop, and establish a presence in the area with hopes of winning NASA contracts. I was nervous; I thought, how will I do this? Maybe I bit off more than I can chew.

But one thing many people know about me is, telling me something cannot be done is like dangling a piece of raw meat in front of a starving dog. I commit to the challenge before I even know why or how I'll go about accomplishing it. After four or five months, I had grown my team to about 10 people, and we soon earned NASA contracts. I personally attended weekly meetings at NASA to see which projects we could help them with. At one such meeting, they needed a way to refurbish large, specialized parabolic mirrors. I said we could do it but needed a particular machine from their naval optics shop. I assured them we would be working within one day of receiving the equipment.

When the equipment arrived, I received a call that maintenance couldn't get the machine through the warehouse door, so I told them to tear the wall down and get the machine running. When NASA came the following day, we were up and running. For another project, NASA needed one hundred atmospheric lenses, which are very tedious to make and would be far too many to make by hand. To achieve this, I designed a new machine, taking an old junky one and changing the spindle inside, inserting indicators for x, y, and z directions. I was successful in creating a machine that could create the precise mirrors that NASA needed.

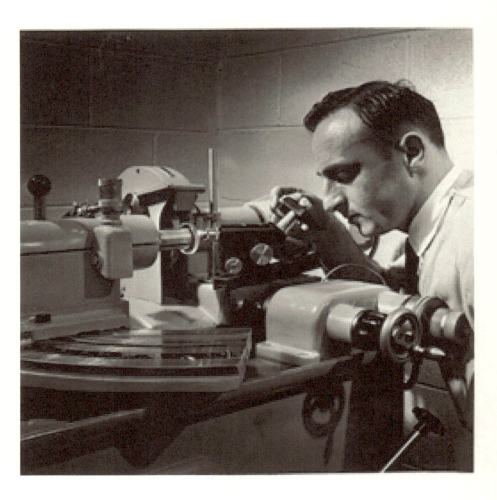

Sol, December 31, 1964

In 1966, after a few of years with Librascope, Perkin Elmer had heard of my accomplishments, and asked me to come in for an interview. They offered me a job. I told them I needed six months to replace myself at Librascope, and they agreed, but only to three months. Somehow, I was never insecure about people taking away my job; I never worried about how I would survive. I knew I would make it.

At Perkin Elmer, I met my colleague Paul Forman. Paul quickly saw what I could do, that I could solve almost any problem, and started a special team to do product development work in which I was in charge. One day, Paul came to me and said NASA needed hundreds of special reflectors to go to the moon, and no one else could do the job. Could we do it? Of course, I said yes. NASA came to see us, and explained they needed 450 prisms made in 6 months. I hand-made six cubes a day, which were then made into 12 prisms.

Through these projects, I was able to revolutionize the production of reliable high precision optical components and prisms. To this day, the leading laser labs in France, Livermore, California, and at the University of Rochester, among others, are pursuing highly ambitious and potentially game-changing programs related to laser fusion and possibly other laser-oriented objectives.

The highly specialized and polished glass components required for laser use in research, along with the equipment used to manufacture and test the polished glass can generally be traced back to my work while at Perkin Elmer. Myself and my colleague Dr. Carl Zanoni, a knowledgeable scientist and engineer, brainstormed solutions to the challenges posed by NASA. I then led the development process, including development of suitable equipment to meet NASA's exacting standards for specifications and quantities.

For example, Apollo 11, Apollo 14 and Apollo 15 carried specialized instrumentation for accurate measurement of the distance between the earth and moon. NASA and other teams of engineers and scientists designed a process that involved placing an array of prism reflectors on the lunar surface and firing laser beams from earth toward the reflectors. The returning laser beams reflected back to earth, where differences in wavelength were used to calculate the distance travelled by the beams. It was successful, in large part due to my team's invention of processes and equipment for the reliable and efficient production and testing of precision optical components and prisms.

In 1970, myself, Paul Forman and Dr. Carl Zanoni, decided we would open our own company, and co-founded Zygo Corporation, a highly specialized optics innovation and manufacturing endeavor. We launched in partnership with Canon Inc. and Wesleyan University, both of which had significant investment and stake in advancing optics research and production. Our inventions and innovations quickly contributed to the advancement of physics, optics, and engineering.

Among our numerous breakthroughs, the Zygo team designed and released the first user-friendly precision interferometer in 1972. Because of our work, processes that had been strictly the domain of engineers could now be trusted to trained line workers on customer assembly lines.

Today, the Zygo team actually manufactures the machines that produces precision optical components to far more intricate specs. They also produce the instrumentation that enables stakeholders to test those components during and after the production process.

From left to right: Dr. Mitarai - President, Canon, Worldwide; Mr. Suzuyawa, Cannon Exec; Sol; Mr. Numaja, Manager, Tamacawa Plant; Mr. Mitsui – President, Canon, USA

Laser Ranger Retro-Reflector, Apollo

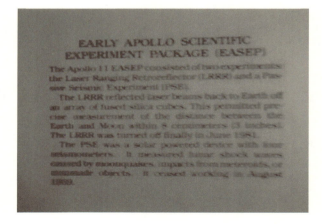

LRRR Exhibit at National Air and Space Museum

CONCLUSION

It has long been known that, in the face of life-threatening trauma and unspeakable loss, our most primitive instincts summon previously-unknown and unimaginable strengths and reserves. The awesome hidden potential of our "lizard brain" is awakened instantaneously. In an instant we are prepared to either fight or flee. We have all heard of the demure mother whose infant is trapped in a burning vehicle following a violent crash. Bloody and in shock, she returns to the car, struggles to open doors or smash windows, but ultimately forces a mangled door open and rescues her child. The first responders are in awe of her ability to accomplish what would ordinarily require pneumatic "jaws of life."

Sol, along with millions of others, experienced and witnessed unspeakable horrors at an early age, over a sustained period, without consolation or reprieve. Alone (emotionally), afraid, and without even a glimmer of hope or promise in sight, they were physically and emotionally incapable of overt, actionable fight or flight.

Behavioral psychologists have written much about this phenomenon called "learned helplessness." In summary, the mouse that gets an electric shock regardless of its behavior ultimately becomes passive and unmotivated to strive for a reward. In essence, when everything we've learned fails, animals become depressed and despondent. They become "helpless" through their own experiences of failure in their surroundings.

In this context, it would follow that the despair and helplessness of adults would be exponentially deeper than children's response to an upside-down universe, where right and wrong, day and night, kind and cruel, pride and prejudice are interchangeable and unpredictable.

Yet for some, like Sol, the sustained trauma served as the conditions for the birth of a perfect storm of inner force that, once summoned and harnessed, yielded a silent, simmering, lasting focus and sustained drive and tenacity that yielded unimaginable successes over a long, healthy, and highly creative lifetime.

Beyond his personal strength, Sol's successes can also be seen through the lives of his grandchildren. Zev Hechtman is Sol's eldest grandson. He is married to his beautiful wife Samantha, and they live in Washington, DC. After graduating from law school and completing his LL.M, Zev moved to Israel where he worked for Ernst & Young. He is currently a senior manager in the tax department of Danaher Corporation. Saba Shlomo (Sol) was an inspiration to Zev; and often served as a catalyst for good in his life. Never one to mince words, Zev will always remember Saba saying of courting Samantha, "Don't be a loser, be a winner!"

Haim Hechtman received a Doctorate in Physical Therapy from Northeastern University in 2007, moved to Washington DC, and co-founded Point Performance in 2014 – a comprehensive physical therapy and physical medicine practice, employing nearly 30 staff and growing. Haim fondly remembers spending time with and learning from Saba, like riding the tractor, fishing in the pond together, and visiting Zygo on weekends. Saba and Savta shared their love of travel with Haim, taking him to Montreal when he was eight years old, and to Israel when he was 11.

Through two mutual friends, a boat, Baltimore Avenue, and the suggestion that "they might get along," Haim and Ariel Moyer were introduced in May of 2015. They quickly formed a life together through travel, adventure and trust. Haim proposed Thanksgiving Day of 2016 and they were married June 2017 at a private ceremony, which Saba and Sadie attended. On September 13, 2018, Sawyer Bear Hechtman joined their family. Saba had the opportunity to virtually attend his *bris*, and to hold him over his 90th birthday weekend. Saba always looked forward to receiving daily photos of his newest great-grandson. Bear will be raised to embody Saba's legacy of family, strength and knowledge.

Aaron is Sol's second oldest grandchild, and lives in Boston with his wife, Elena, and their two beautiful children, Benjamin (2013) and Mia (2016). Sol was so proud to have great grandchildren and often pulled Aaron and Elena aside to say thank you, "for giving me great grandchildren." Sol was especially close with the oldest, Benjamin, who upon arrival would be asked immediately to sit on his lap so Sol could tell him, "I love you, I love you." Benjamin too feels a deep connection with his "Saba G," and like his father and Sol, shares a love for science, math, and problem solving. Aaron, who graduated from Northeastern University with a degree in Chemical Engineering, attributes his success as an adult, both personally and professionally, to his Saba, who taught him to always push forward, no matter the circumstance. It is important to both Aaron and Elena that this lesson be carried onto the next generation, not just through stories, but actions. Aaron and Elena will forever cherish the time spent with Saba, Sadie and their kids over the years as they shared a lot of laughs, love, wisdom and kindness. Sol will stay in their hearts forever.

Adam is Sol's middle grandson. Sol was always analytical in the way he approached both life and work, but there stood a soft side and touch to how he went about this. Many times, while Adam was in high school, Sol would pull him aside and start to discuss his future. True to Sol, the inevitable business side of the discussion dominated, but one conversation vividly stood out to Adam. Sol broke from the usual, "you have to study hard and work hard if you are to succeed," and stressed that the true key to success is respect; if you don't have respect for people, people won't have respect for you. He then proceeded to make Adam look him in the eyes and spell it out: R.E.S.P.E.C.T. Adam never forgot this

Aretha Franklin moment with his Saba and to this day uses this simple mantra to shape his life and career.

Jacob, an engineer and problem solver like Sol, cherishes many memories and lessons from his Saba. Jacob fondly remembers early morning walks around the pond and property in Middletown, Connecticut, exploring nature and discussing a wide array of topics. Creativity, perseverance and hard work were a few of the lesson that Saba taught his grandson from an early age. Philosophy was always a matter of discussion and a cornerstone in many lessons for as long as Jacob can remember. Even the simple task of catching a fish was not complete without a full understanding of how life turned to death turned to dinner.

Alisa, or 'Quicksilver' as her Saba called her, is Sol's youngest grandchild. She lives in Washington DC, where she currently works as a contract employee for the U.S. Department of State's Bureau of International Security and

Non-proliferation. Her Saba taught her his mantra, "If there's a will there's a way," at a young age – and it has inspired her to chase after her aspirations of pursuing the path of public service and international security ever since. Some of her fondest memories of her grandfather include building a bridge across a creek with him at his Middletown house, and being taught how to concentrate, a lesson that Sol gave by showing her how to refrain from laughing while being tickled. When friends visit her in DC, one of Alisa's favorite places to take them is to the National Air and Space Museum so she can show them the Laser Ranger Retro-Reflector that her Saba helped create during his time at Zygo.

EDITOR'S NOTE

On Friday, December 7, 2018, Sol passed away at the age of ninety years old, with his wife, Sadie Rudman Laufer by his side. Sol met Sadie some years after Betty passed away of pancreatic cancer. Sol and Sadie's rabbi, Rabbi Steinmetz introduced them, and the rest is history.

Sol's three children, Rachel and her husband Andy, Orna and her husband Jim, and Jonah and his wife Pam, gave him six grandchildren, Zev, Haim, Adam, Aaron, Jacob and Alisa; three great-grandchildren, Benjamin, Mia, and Sawyer Bear, and another on the way. Together with Sadie's family, who loved Sol as their own, Sol built a life with a family he loves, and of which he is endlessly proud.

Though his story must be told so the generations to come will never forget the atrocities of the Holocaust, even until the day he died, after all he had been through, Sol blamed no one for his suffering. He did not claim to be a victim. He carried no ill-will, no hate, or anger; only pride in what he has accomplished and created of his life, in spite of it all. Sol turned a childhood of suffering into a lifetime of thriving, and no one could take that away from him.

APPENDIX

TIMELINE OF WORLD WAR II MILESTONES

1933

According to the census of June 16, 1933, the Jewish population of Germany, including the Saar region (which at that time was still under the administration of the League of Nations), was approximately 505,000 people out of a total population of 67 million, or somewhat less than 0.75 percent. That number represented a reduction from the estimated 523,000 Jews living in Germany in January 1933; the decrease was due in part to emigration following the Nazi takeover in January. An estimated 37,000 Jews emigrated from Germany during 1933.

1938

German Troops Invade Austria and Incorporate Austria into the German Reich in what is known as the Anschluss. Germany absorbs Austria, Sudetenland Anschluss.

1939

Germany Invades Poland, Starting World War II. Britain.. France Declare War on Germany.

Sol is 11 years of age

1940

Germany invades Norway, Denmark, Belgium and the Netherlands.   Bombing of Britain Begins.

1941

Germany invades the Soviet Union. Japan bombs Pearl Harbor.   U.S. Declares War on Japan.

June 1944

D-day: Allied troops land in France.

May 8, 1945

Germany surrenders.
Sol is 16 in May.

THE BEGINNING OF THE END: THIRD REICH ANTISEMITIC LEGISLATION

During the first six years of Hitler's dictatorship, government at every level — Reich, state and municipal — adopted hundreds of laws, decrees, directives, guidelines, and regulations that increasingly restricted the civil and human rights of the Jews in Germany.
Here are examples of anti-Jewish legislation in Nazi Germany, 1933–1939:

1933
March 31
Decree of the Berlin city commissioner for health suspends Jewish doctors from the city's charity services.

April 7
Law for the Reestablishment of the Professional Civil Service removes Jews from government service.

April 7
Law on the Admission to the Legal Profession forbids the admission of Jews to the bar.

April 25
Law against Overcrowding in Schools and Universities limits the number of Jewish students in public schools.

July 14
De-Naturalization Law revokes the citizenship of naturalized Jews and "undesirables."

October 4
Law on Editors bans Jews from editorial posts.

1935
May 21
Army law expels Jewish officers from the army.

September 15
Nazi leaders announce the Nuremberg Laws.

1936
January 11
Executive Order on the Reich Tax Law forbids Jews to serve as tax-consultants.

April 3
Reich Veterinarians Law expels Jews from the veterinary profession.

October 15

Reich Ministry of Education bans Jewish teachers from public schools.

1937
April 9
The Mayor of Berlin orders public schools not to admit Jewish children until further notice.

1938
January 5
Law on the Alteration of Family and Personal Names forbids Jews from changing their names.

February 5
Law on the Profession of Auctioneer excludes Jews from this occupation.

March 18
The Gun Law excludes Jewish gun merchants.

April 22
Decree against the Camouflage of Jewish Firms forbids changing the names of Jewish-owned businesses.

April 26
Order for the Disclosure of Jewish Assets requires Jews to report all property in excess of 5,000 Reichsmarks.

July 11
Reich Ministry of the Interior bans Jews from health spas.

August 17
Executive Order on the Law on the Alteration of Family and Personal Names requires Jews to adopt an additional name: "Sara" for women and "Israel" for men.

October 3
Decree on the Confiscation of Jewish Property regulates the transfer of assets from Jews to non-Jewish Germans.

October 5
The Reich Interior Ministry invalidates all German passports held by Jews. Jews must surrender their old passports, which will become valid only after the letter "J" had been stamped on them.

November 12
Decree on the Exclusion of Jews from German Economic Life closes all Jewish-owned businesses.

November 15
Reich Ministry of Education expels all Jewish children from public schools.

November 28
Reich Ministry of Interior restricts the freedom of movement of Jews.

November 29
The Reich Interior Ministry forbids Jews to keep carrier pigeons.

December 14
An Executive Order on the Law on the Organization of National Work cancels all state contracts held with Jewish-owned firms.

December 21
Law on Midwives bans all Jews from the occupation.

1939
February 21
Decree Concerning the Surrender of Precious Metals and Stones in Jewish Ownership.

August 1
The President of the German Lottery forbids the sale of lottery tickets to Jews.

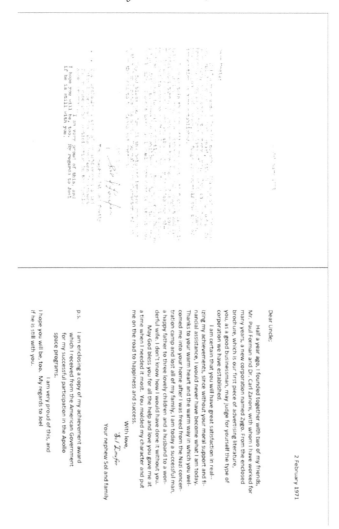

2 February 1971

Dear Uncle:

Half a year ago, I founded together with two of my friends, Mr. Paul Forman and Dr. Carl Zanoni, with whom I have worked for many years, a new corporation named Zygo. From the enclosed brochure, which is our first piece of advertising literature, you, as a good businessman, may judge for yourself the type of corporation we have established.

I am certain that you will have great satisfaction in realizing my achievements, since without your moral support and financial assistance, I would never have become what I am today. Thanks to your warm heart and the warm way in which you welcomed me into your home after I was freed from the Nazi concentration camp and lost all of my family, I am today a successful man, a happy father to three lovely children and a husband to a wonderful wife. I don't know how I would have done it without you.

May God bless you for all the help and love you gave me at a time when I needed it most. You molded my character and put me on the road to happiness and success.

With love,

Your nephew Sol and family

p.s.   I am enclosing a copy of my achievement award which I received from the American Government for my successful participation in the Apollo space programs.

I am very proud of this, and

I hope you will be, too. My regards to Joel if he is still with you.

October 11, 1995

To our dear children,

SHALOM!!!

I know that you are interested in hearing more about our trip to eastern Europe, especially my personal experience. The write-up you already received summarizes some of it. Prague was very beautiful and we hope to visit there again. Budapest was so-so, with one visit being enough. Lithuania was very sad. As to Poland, we looked upon it as a large Jewish cemetery, and it was not considered a vacation. I was fully aware that this trip was going to be very painful and difficult for me personally. However, I never imagined it to be so stressful, and deeply and intensively painful. During our short time in Poland, especially at Auschwitz, I relived four to five years of bad memories of misery and suffering in just a few days. It was not easy for me.

When the war broke out I was only eleven years old. At the age of fourteen I had been taken to a concentration working camp (lucky me), and this was the last time I had seen my entire family. In those days I was too young to fully comprehend the severity and magnitude of the holocaust. The extreme suffering and the terror my parents had to endure. How terrified they must have been while walking into the gas chamber with their two little boys alongside of them. I will always wonder what their last words were.

More than one month has passed since we visited Auschwitz, and the sight of it and what happened is still with me. I can not take it off my mind, and am still in the state of bereavement as if it is my mourning period. It was my duty to be there and I wish that I had made this trip many years ago. I never could attend my parents funeral, nor have I ever seen their burial place because there is none. We walked silently in grief, with many angry feelings, through the dark, long buildings and barracks which today is the Auschwitz Museum. What we had seen there was very shocking and heartbreaking. There were huge piles of adults and childrens shoes, piles of toothbrushes, combs, and eyeglasses, tons of human hair, and mountains of the victims luggage with their names marked on it. And, the walls are covered with testimony of the darkest period in human history. The horror of Auschwitz should be engraved on the face of each German living today as a reminder to the future generations of the awful, horrible crimes their parents and grandparents, who called themselves "Nazi's", the brutal murderers, perpetrated.

Among the sad, depressing, and painful surroundings of Auschwitz, we saw a ray of shining, bright light. We came across a few large groups of beautiful and proud Israeli teenagers all wearing large Star of David's on the front and back of their shirts, with large Israel flags in their hands. They too were exploring the past. **BUT THEY ARE THE FUTURE!!!** May they grow in strength and live in peace among their neighbors.

Thank God that we are all healthy. We had a wonderful holiday and are looking forward to a bright and happy future for our whole family, and all our friends. As you know, on October 15 we will be departing for Sarasota, Florida where we rented a small villa to stay for four weeks. The address and phone number where we can be reached during this time is below. During this time we will be busy finalizing our new winter home with the builder, architect, and interior designer/decorator. We hope to start building by December 1995.

In 1996 we plan to spend four to five months in Florida in our new home. You are all welcome to join us there! We hope you will visit!

With our best wishes and love to all of you,

Mom & Dad

17155871R00072

17155871R00072

Made in United States
Troutdale, OR
01/25/2024

17155871R00072